MznLnx

Missing Links Exam Preps

Exam Prep for

Foundations in Strategic Management

Harrison & St. John, 4th Edition

The MznLnx Exam Prep is your link from the texbook and lecture to your exams.
The MznLnx Exam Preps are unauthorized and comprehensive reviews of your textbooks.

All material provided by MznLnx and Rico Publications (c) 2010
Textbook publishers and textbook authors do not particpate in or contribute to these reviews.

MznLnx

Rico Publications

Exam Prep for Foundations in Strategic Management
4th Edition
Harrison & St. John

Publisher: Raymond Houge
Assistant Editor: Michael Rouger
Text and Cover Designer: Lisa Buckner
Marketing Manager: Sara Swagger
Project Manager, Editorial Production: Jerry Emerson
Art Director: Vernon Lowerui

Product Manager: Dave Mason
Editorial Assitant: Rachel Guzmanji
Pedagogy: Debra Long
Cover Image: Jim Reed/Getty Images
Text and Cover Printer: City Printing, Inc.
Compositor: Media Mix, Inc.

(c) 2010 Rico Publications
ALL RIGHTS RESERVED. No part of this work covered by the copyright may be reproduced or used in any form or by an means--graphic, electronic, or mechanical, including photocopying, recording, taping, Web distribution, information storage, and retrieval systems, or in any other manner--without the written permission of the publisher.

Printed in the United States
ISBN:

For more information about our products, contact us at:
Dave.Mason@RicoPublications.com

For permission to use material from this text or product, submit a request online to:
Dave.Mason@RicoPublications.com

Contents

CHAPTER 1
The Strategic Management Process — 1
CHAPTER 2
The External Environment — 7
CHAPTER 3
Organizational Resources and Competitive Advantage — 15
CHAPTER 4
Strategic Direction — 29
CHAPTER 5
Business-Level Strategies — 33
CHAPTER 6
Corporate Strategies — 41
CHAPTER 7
Strategy Implementation — 46
CHAPTER 8
Strategic Control and Restructuring — 55
ANSWER KEY — 65

TO THE STUDENT

COMPREHENSIVE

The *MznLnx* Exam Prep series is designed to help you pass your exams. Editors at MznLnx review your textbooks and then prepare these practice exams to help you master the textbook material. Unlike study guides, workbooks, and practice tests provided by the texbook publisher and textbook authors, *MznLnx* gives you **all** of the material in each chapter in exam form, not just samples, so you can be sure to nail your exam.

MECHANICAL

The MznLnx Exam Prep series creates exams that will help you learn the subject matter as well as test you on your understanding. Each question is designed to help you master the concept. Just working through the exams, you gain an understanding of the subject--its a simple mechanical process that produces success.

INTEGRATED STUDY GUIDE AND REVIEW

MznLnx is not just a set of exams designed to test you, its also a comprehensive review of the subject content. Each exam question is also a review of the concept, making sure that you will get the answer correct without having to go to other sources of material. You learn as you go! Its the easiest way to pass an exam.

HUMOR

Studying can be tedious and dry. MznLnx's instructional design includes moderate humor within the exam questions on occassion, to break the tedium and revitalize the brain

Chapter 1. The Strategic Management Process 1

1. _____ is the state of being which occurs when a person, object, or service is no longer wanted even though it may still be in good working order. _____ frequently occurs because a replacement has become available that is superior in one or more aspects. Videotapes making way for DVDs

Technical _____ may occur when a new product or technology supersedes the old, and it becomes preferred to utilize the new technology in place of the old.

   a. A Stake in the Outcome
   b. A4e
   c. AAAI
   d. Obsolescence

2. _____ is the process of estimation in unknown situations. Prediction is a similar, but more general term. Both can refer to estimation of time series, cross-sectional or longitudinal data.
   a. 33 Strategies of War
   b. 1990 Clean Air Act
   c. Forecasting
   d. 28-hour day

3. In general, a _____ is an arrangement to provide people with an income when they are no longer earning a regular income from employment.

The terms retirement plan or superannuation refer to a _____ granted upon retirement . Retirement plans may be set up by employers, insurance companies, the government or other institutions such as employer associations or trade unions.

   a. Wage
   b. Pension
   c. State Compensation Insurance Fund
   d. Pension insurance contract

4. _____ is a strategic planning method used to evaluate the Strengths, Weaknesses, Opportunities, and Threats involved in a project or in a business venture. It involves specifying the objective of the business venture or project and identifying the internal and external factors that are favorable and unfavorable to achieving that objective. The technique is credited to Albert Humphrey, who led a convention at Stanford University in the 1960s and 1970s using data from Fortune 500 companies.

Chapter 1. The Strategic Management Process

   a. Marketing
   b. Corporate image
   c. SWOT analysis
   d. Market share

5. _____ is, in very basic words, a position a firm occupies against its competitors.

According to Michael Porter, the three methods for creating a sustainable _____ are through:

1. Cost leadership

2. Differentiation

3. Focus (economics)

   a. 28-hour day
   b. Competitive Advantage
   c. Theory Z
   d. 1990 Clean Air Act

6. _____ refers to the aggregated strategies of single business firm or a strategic business unit (SBU) in a diversified corporation. According to Michael Porter, a firm must formulate a _____ that incorporates either cost leadership, differentiation or focus in order to achieve a sustainable competitive advantage and long-term success in its chosen arenas or industries.

Functional strategies include marketing strategies, new product development strategies, human resource strategies, financial strategies, legal strategies, supply-chain strategies, and information technology management strategies.

   a. Strategic thinking
   b. Competitive heterogeneity
   c. Business strategy
   d. Switching cost

7. _____ is an organization's process of defining its strategy and making decisions on allocating its resources to pursue this strategy, including its capital and people. Various business analysis techniques can be used in _____, including SWOT analysis (Strengths, Weaknesses, Opportunities, and Threats) and PEST analysis (Political, Economic, Social, and Technological analysis) or STEER analysis involving Socio-cultural, Technological, Economic, Ecological, and Regulatory factors and EPISTEL (Environment, Political, Informatic, Social, Technological, Economic and Legal)

_____ is the formal consideration of an organization's future course. All _____ deals with at least one of three key questions:

1. 'What do we do?'
2. 'For whom do we do it?'
3. 'How do we excel?'

In business _____, the third question is better phrased 'How can we beat or avoid competition?'. (Bradford and Duncan, page 1.)

   a. Strategic planning
   b. 1990 Clean Air Act
   c. 33 Strategies of War
   d. 28-hour day

8. A _____ is a brief written statement of the purpose of a company or organization. Ideally, a _____ guides the actions of the organization, spells out its overall goal, provides a sense of direction, and guides decision making for all levels of management.

_____s often contain the following:

- Purpose and aim of the organization
- The organization's primary stakeholders: clients, stockholders, etc.
- Responsibilities of the organization toward these stakeholders
- Products and services offered

In developing a _____.

- Encourage as much input as feasible from employees, volunteers, and other stakeholders
- Publicize it broadly

The _____ can be used to resolve differences between business stakeholders. Stakeholders include: employees including managers and executives, stockholders, board of directors, customers, suppliers, distributors, creditors, governments (local, state, federal, etc.), unions, competitors, NGO's, and the general public.

   a. Mission statement
   b. 33 Strategies of War
   c. 1990 Clean Air Act
   d. 28-hour day

Chapter 1. The Strategic Management Process

9. The _____ is an economic tool used to determine the strategic resources available to a firm. The fundamental principle of the _____ is that the basis for a competitive advantage of a firm lies primarily in the application of the bundle of valuable resources at the firm's disposal (Wernerfelt, 1984, p172; Rumelt, 1984, p557-558.) To transform a short-run competitive advantage into a sustained competitive advantage requires that these resources are heterogeneous in nature and not perfectly mobile (Barney, 1991, p105-106; Peteraf, 1993, p180).

   a. Business philosophy
   b. Frenemy
   c. Resource-based view
   d. Catfish effect

10. _____ is a term used in project management and business administration to describe a process where all the individuals or groups that are likely to be affected by the activities of a project are identified and then sorted according to how much they can affect the project and how much the project can affect them. This information is used to assess how the interests of those stakeholders should be addressed in the project plan.

   A stakeholder is any person or organization, who can be positively or negatively impacted by, or cause an impact on the actions of a company.

   a. 28-hour day
   b. 1990 Clean Air Act
   c. 33 Strategies of War
   d. Stakeholder analysis

11. Competitive advantage is, in very basic words, a position a firm occupies against its competitors.

    According to Michael Porter, the three methods for creating a _____ are through:

    1. Cost leadership - Cost advantage occurs when a firm delivers the same services as its competitors but at a lower cost;

    2.

   a. 1990 Clean Air Act
   b. 28-hour day
   c. Sustainable competitive advantage
   d. Theory Z

Chapter 1. The Strategic Management Process 5

12. The United Nations _____ is an United Nations initiative to encourage businesses worldwide to adopt sustainable and socially responsible policies, and to report on their implementation. The _____ is a principle based framework for businesses, stating ten principles in the areas of human rights, labour, the environment and anti-corruption. Under the _____, companies are brought together with UN agencies, labour groups and civil society.

   a. 33 Strategies of War
   b. 28-hour day
   c. 1990 Clean Air Act
   d. Global Compact

13. _____ in its literal sense is the process of transformation of local or regional phenomena into global ones. It can be described as a process by which the people of the world are unified into a single society and function together.

This process is a combination of economic, technological, sociocultural and political forces.

   a. Cost Management
   b. Globalization
   c. Histogram
   d. Collaborative Planning, Forecasting and Replenishment

14. _____ is an area of knowledge within organizational theory that studies models and theories about the way an organization learns and adapts.

In Organizational development (OD), learning is a characteristic of an adaptive organization, i.e., an organization that is able to sense changes in signals from its environment (both internal and external) and adapt accordingly.

   a. AAAI
   b. A Stake in the Outcome
   c. A4e
   d. Organizational learning

15. Recent strategic thought points ever more clearly towards the conclusion that the critical strategic question is not 'What?,' but 'Why?' The work of Mintzberg and others who draw a distinction between strategic planning (defined as systematic programming of pre-identified strategies) and _____ supports that conclusion. Intensified exploration of strategy from new directions is now coming together in the concept of what is being called _____. At this point, there is no generally accepted definition of the term, no common agreement as to its role or importance, and no standardized list of key competencies of strategic thinkers.

Chapter 1. The Strategic Management Process

   a. Strategic drift
   b. Switching cost
   c. Complementors
   d. Strategic thinking

16. The _____ of 2002 (Pub.L. 107-204, 116 Stat. 745, enacted July 30, 2002), also known as the Public Company Accounting Reform and Investor Protection Act of 2002 and commonly called Sarbanes-Oxley, Sarbox or SOX, is a United States federal law enacted on July 30, 2002, as a reaction to a number of major corporate and accounting scandals including those affecting Enron, Tyco International, Adelphia, Peregrine Systems and WorldCom.
   a. Sarbanes-Oxley Act of 2002
   b. Letter of credit
   c. Sarbanes-Oxley Act
   d. Fair Labor Standards Act

17. The _____, also known as the Public Company Accounting Reform and Investor Protection Act of 2002 and commonly called Sarbanes-Oxley, Sarbox or SOX, is a United States federal law enacted on July 30, 2002, as a reaction to a number of major corporate and accounting scandals including those affecting Enron, Tyco International, Adelphia, Peregrine Systems and WorldCom.
   a. Sarbanes-Oxley Act of 2002
   b. Munn v. Illinois
   c. MacPherson v. Buick Motor Co.
   d. Letter of credit

18. In economics, _____ is the desire to own something and the ability to pay for it. The term _____ signifies the ability or the willingness to buy a particular commodity at a given point of time.
   a. 33 Strategies of War
   b. 1990 Clean Air Act
   c. 28-hour day
   d. Demand

Chapter 2. The External Environment

1. _____ is a concept in ethics with several meanings. It is often used synonymously with such concepts as responsibility, answerability, enforcement, blameworthiness, liability and other terms associated with the expectation of account-giving. As an aspect of governance, it has been central to discussions related to problems in both the public and private (corporation) worlds.
   a. Usury
   b. Accountability
   c. A4e
   d. A Stake in the Outcome

2. _____ is an advertisement in which a particular product specifically mentions a competitor by name for the express purpose of showing why the competitor is inferior to the product naming it.

This should not be confused with parody advertisements, where a fictional product is being advertised for the purpose of poking fun at the particular advertisement, nor should it be confused with the use of a coined brand name for the purpose of comparing the product without actually naming an actual competitor. ('Wikipedia tastes better and is less filling than the Encyclopedia Galactica.')

In the 1980s, during what has been referred to as the cola wars, soft-drink manufacturer Pepsi ran a series of advertisements where people, caught on hidden camera, in a blind taste test, chose Pepsi over rival Coca-Cola.

   a. 33 Strategies of War
   b. 1990 Clean Air Act
   c. 28-hour day
   d. Comparative advertising

3. _____ is the process of estimation in unknown situations. Prediction is a similar, but more general term. Both can refer to estimation of time series, cross-sectional or longitudinal data.
   a. 1990 Clean Air Act
   b. Forecasting
   c. 28-hour day
   d. 33 Strategies of War

4. The _____ of 2002 (Pub.L. 107-204, 116 Stat. 745, enacted July 30, 2002), also known as the Public Company Accounting Reform and Investor Protection Act of 2002 and commonly called Sarbanes-Oxley, Sarbox or SOX, is a United States federal law enacted on July 30, 2002, as a reaction to a number of major corporate and accounting scandals including those affecting Enron, Tyco International, Adelphia, Peregrine Systems and WorldCom.

Chapter 2. The External Environment

a. Sarbanes-Oxley Act
b. Sarbanes-Oxley Act of 2002
c. Letter of credit
d. Fair Labor Standards Act

5. The _____, also known as the Public Company Accounting Reform and Investor Protection Act of 2002 and commonly called Sarbanes-Oxley, Sarbox or SOX, is a United States federal law enacted on July 30, 2002, as a reaction to a number of major corporate and accounting scandals including those affecting Enron, Tyco International, Adelphia, Peregrine Systems and WorldCom.
   a. MacPherson v. Buick Motor Co.
   b. Letter of credit
   c. Munn v. Illinois
   d. Sarbanes-Oxley Act of 2002

6. In finance, the _____s between two currencies specifies how much one currency is worth in terms of the other. It is the value of a foreign nation's currency in terms of the home nation's currency. For example an _____ of 102 Japanese yen to the United States dollar means that JPY 102 is worth the same as USD 1.
   a. Exchange rate
   b. A Stake in the Outcome
   c. A4e
   d. AAAI

7. In economics, _____ is a rise in the general level of prices of goods and services in an economy over a period of time. When the general price level rises, each unit of the functional currency buys fewer goods and services; consequently, _____ is a decline in the real value of money--a loss of purchasing power in the internal medium of exchange which is also the monetary unit of account in an economy. A chief measure of general price-level _____ is the general _____ rate, which is the percentage change in a general price index (normally the Consumer Price Index) over time.
   a. A4e
   b. A Stake in the Outcome
   c. Economy
   d. Inflation

8. A _____ is a type of business entity in which partners (owners) share with each other the profits or losses of the business. _____s are often favored over corporations for taxation purposes, as the _____ structure does not generally incur a tax on profits before it is distributed to the partners (i.e. there is no dividend tax levied.) However, depending on the _____ structure and the jurisdiction in which it operates, owners of a _____ may be exposed to greater personal liability than they would as shareholders of a corporation.

Chapter 2. The External Environment

a. Mediation
b. Federal Employers Liability Act
c. Partnership
d. Due process

9. _____ is technology based on biology, especially when used in agriculture, food science, and medicine. United Nations Convention on Biological Diversity defines _____ as:

_____ is often used to refer to genetic engineering technology of the 21st century, however the term encompasses a wider range and history of procedures for modifying biological organisms according to the needs of humanity, going back to the initial modifications of native plants into improved food crops through artificial selection and hybridization. Bioengineering is the science upon which all biotechnological applications are based.

a. 33 Strategies of War
b. Biotechnology
c. 1990 Clean Air Act
d. 28-hour day

10. The _____ is an agency of the United States Department of Health and Human Services and is responsible for regulating and supervising the safety of foods, dietary supplements, drugs, vaccines, biological medical products, blood products, medical devices, radiation-emitting devices, veterinary products, and cosmetics. The FDA also enforces section 361 of the Public Health Service Act and the associated regulations, including sanitation requirements on interstate travel as well as specific rules for control of disease on products ranging from pet turtles to semen donations for assisted reproductive medicine techniques.

The FDA is an agency within the United States Department of Health and Human Services responsible for protecting and promoting the nation's public health.

a. 1990 Clean Air Act
b. 33 Strategies of War
c. 28-hour day
d. Food and Drug Administration

11. _____ is a cross-disciplinary area concerned with protecting the safety, health and welfare of people engaged in work or employment. The goal of all _____ programs is to foster a work free safe environment. As a secondary effect, it may also protect co-workers, family members, employers, customers, suppliers, nearby communities, and other members of the public who are impacted by the workplace environment.

a. Occupational Safety and Health
b. A Stake in the Outcome
c. AAAI
d. A4e

12. The United States _____ is an agency of the United States Department of Labor. It was created by Congress under the Occupational Safety and Health Act, signed by President Richard M. Nixon, on December 29, 1970. Its mission is to prevent work-related injuries, illnesses, and deaths by issuing and enforcing rules (called standards) for workplace safety and health.
    a. Opinion leadership
    b. Unemployment insurance
    c. Operant conditioning
    d. Occupational Safety and Health Administration

13. In economics, _____ is the desire to own something and the ability to pay for it. The term _____ signifies the ability or the willingness to buy a particular commodity at a given point of time.
    a. Demand
    b. 1990 Clean Air Act
    c. 28-hour day
    d. 33 Strategies of War

14. _____ is the incidence or process of transferring ownership of a business, enterprise, agency or public service from the public sector (government) to the private sector (business.) In a broader sense, _____ refers to transfer of any government function to the private sector including governmental functions like revenue collection and law enforcement.
    a. Privatization
    b. Performance reports
    c. 28-hour day
    d. 1990 Clean Air Act

15. In economics, _____ is a measure of the relative satisfaction from consumption of various goods and services. Given this measure, one may speak meaningfully of increasing or decreasing _____, and thereby explain economic behavior in terms of attempts to increase one's _____. For illustrative purposes, changes in _____ are sometimes expressed in units called utils.

a. A Stake in the Outcome
b. Utility
c. Ordinal utility
d. Indirect utility function

16. _____ is, in very basic words, a position a firm occupies against its competitors.

According to Michael Porter, the three methods for creating a sustainable _____ are through:

1. Cost leadership

2. Differentiation

3. Focus (economics)

　a. Theory Z
　b. 1990 Clean Air Act
　c. 28-hour day
　d. Competitive Advantage

17. In probability theory, a probability distribution is called _____ if its cumulative distribution function is _____. This is equivalent to saying that for random variables X with the distribution in question, Pr[X = a] = 0 for all real numbers a, i.e.: the probability that X attains the value a is zero, for any number a. If the distribution of X is _____ then X is called a _____ random variable.
　a. Pay Band
　b. Connectionist expert systems
　c. Decision tree pruning
　d. Continuous

18. A _____ is a concept used in strategic management that groups companies within an industry that have similar business models or similar combinations of strategies. For example, the restaurant industry can be divided into several _____s including fast-food and fine-dining based on variables such as preparation time, pricing, and presentation. The number of groups within an industry and their composition depends on the dimensions used to define the groups.
　a. Strategic business unit
　b. Strategic drift
　c. Strategic group
　d. Corporate strategy

Chapter 2. The External Environment

19. _____ consists of the sale of goods or merchandise from a fixed location, such as a department store, boutique or kiosk in small or individual lots for direct consumption by the purchaser. _____ may include subordinated services, such as delivery. Purchasers may be individuals or businesses.
   a. 28-hour day
   b. 1990 Clean Air Act
   c. Planogram
   d. Retailing

20. _____ is the use of control systems (such as numerical control, programmable logic control, and other industrial control systems), in concert with other applications of information technology (such as computer-aided technologies [CAD, CAM, CAx]), to control industrial machinery and processes, reducing the need for human intervention. In the scope of industrialization, _____ is a step beyond mechanization. Whereas mechanization provided human operators with machinery to assist them with the physical requirements of work, _____ greatly reduces the need for human sensory and mental requirements as well.
   a. Automation
   b. A4e
   c. AAAI
   d. A Stake in the Outcome

21. _____ is a legally declared inability or impairment of ability of an individual or organization to pay its creditors. Creditors may file a _____ petition against a debtor ('involuntary _____') in an effort to recoup a portion of what they are owed or initiate a restructuring. In the majority of cases, however, _____ is initiated by the debtor (a 'voluntary _____' that is filed by the insolvent individual or organization.)
   a. 1990 Clean Air Act
   b. 28-hour day
   c. Bankruptcy
   d. 33 Strategies of War

22. _____ is an agreement, usually secretive, which occurs between two or more persons to deceive, mislead or to obtain an objective forbidden by law typically involving fraud or gaining an unfair advantage. It is an agreement among firms to divide the market, set prices kickbacks, or misrepresenting the independence of the relationship between the colluding parties.' All acts effected by _____ are considered void.
   a. Predatory pricing
   b. 1990 Clean Air Act
   c. 28-hour day
   d. Collusion

Chapter 2. The External Environment

23. A _____ is a formal relationship between two or more parties to pursue a set of agreed upon goals or to meet a critical business need while remaining independent organizations.

Partners may provide the _____ with resources such as products, distribution channels, manufacturing capability, project funding, capital equipment, knowledge, expertise, or intellectual property. The alliance is a cooperation or collaboration which aims for a synergy where each partner hopes that the benefits from the alliance will be greater than those from individual efforts.

   a. Golden parachute
   b. Strategic alliance
   c. Farmshoring
   d. Process automation

24. _____ is the advantage gained by the initial occupant of a market segment. This advantage may stem from the fact that the first entrant can gain control of resources that followers may not be able to match. Sometimes the first mover is not able to capitalise on its advantage, leaving the opportunity for another firm to gain second-mover advantage.

   a. Customer retention
   b. Horizontal integration
   c. First-mover advantage
   d. Business ecosystem

25. A _____ or transnational corporation is a corporation or enterprise that manages production or delivers services in more than one country. It can also be referred to as an international corporation.

The first modern _____ is generally thought to be the Dutch East India Company, established in 1602.

   a. Multinational corporation
   b. Command center
   c. Financial Accounting Standards Board
   d. Small and medium enterprises

26. A _____ is a general term that describes any government policy or regulation that restricts international trade. The barriers can take many forms, including the following terms that include many restrictions in international trade within multiple countries that import and export any items of trade.

- Import duty
- Import licenses
- Export licenses
- Import quotas
- Tariffs
- Subsidies
- Non-tariff barriers to trade
- Voluntary Export Restraints
- Local Content Requirements
- Embargo

Most _____s work on the same principle: the imposition of some sort of cost on trade that raises the price of the traded products. If two or more nations repeatedly use _____s against each other, then a trade war results.

a. Trade barrier
b. Customs brokerage
c. Trade creation
d. Most favoured nation

Chapter 3. Organizational Resources and Competitive Advantage

1. _____ is, in very basic words, a position a firm occupies against its competitors.

According to Michael Porter, the three methods for creating a sustainable _____ are through:

1. Cost leadership

2. Differentiation

3. Focus (economics)

   a. 28-hour day
   b. 1990 Clean Air Act
   c. Competitive advantage
   d. Theory Z

2. _____ is a legally declared inability or impairment of ability of an individual or organization to pay its creditors. Creditors may file a _____ petition against a debtor ('involuntary _____') in an effort to recoup a portion of what they are owed or initiate a restructuring. In the majority of cases, however, _____ is initiated by the debtor (a 'voluntary _____' that is filed by the insolvent individual or organization.)
   a. Bankruptcy
   b. 1990 Clean Air Act
   c. 33 Strategies of War
   d. 28-hour day

3. _____ is something that a firm can do well and that meets the following three conditions:

Competencies are things that companys execute well across several business units or product sectors.

Firms usually have few competencies, but these are usually less liable to change rapidly.

   1. It provides consumer benefits
   2. It is not easy for competitors to imitate
   3. It can be leveraged widely to many products and markets.

A _____ can take various forms, including technical/subject matter know-how, a reliable process and/or close relationships with customers and suppliers (Mascarenhas et al. 1998.)

Chapter 3. Organizational Resources and Competitive Advantage

   a. Dominant Design
   b. Learning-by-doing
   c. NAIRU
   d. Core competency

4. _____ is an increasingly broadening term with which an organization, or other human system describes the combination of traditionally administrative personnel functions with acquisition and application of skills, knowledge and experience, Employee Relations and resource planning at various levels. The field draws upon concepts developed in Industrial/Organizational Psychology and System Theory. _____ has at least two related interpretations depending on context. The original usage derives from political economy and economics, where it was traditionally called labor, one of four factors of production although this perspective is changing as a function of new and ongoing research into more strategic approaches at national levels. This first usage is used more in terms of '_____ development', and can go beyond just organizations to the level of nations . The more traditional usage within corporations and businesses refers to the individuals within a firm or agency, and to the portion of the organization that deals with hiring, firing, training, and other personnel issues, typically referred to as `_____ management'.
   a. Human resource management
   b. Human resources
   c. Progressive discipline
   d. Bradford Factor

5. _____ refers to the process of screening, and selecting qualified people for a job at an organization or firm mid- and large-size organizations and companies often retain professional recruiters or outsource some of the process to _____ agencies. External _____ is the process of attracting and selecting employees from outside the organization.

The _____ industry has four main types of agencies: employment agencies, _____ websites and job search engines, 'headhunters' for executive and professional _____, and in-house _____.

   a. Referral recruitment
   b. Recruitment Process Outsourcing
   c. Labour hire
   d. Recruitment

6. _____ is the process of estimation in unknown situations. Prediction is a similar, but more general term. Both can refer to estimation of time series, cross-sectional or longitudinal data.

Chapter 3. Organizational Resources and Competitive Advantage   17

a. 1990 Clean Air Act
b. Forecasting
c. 33 Strategies of War
d. 28-hour day

7. A _____ or chief executive is one of the highest-ranking corporate officer (executive) or administrator in charge of total management. An individual selected as President and _____ of a corporation, company, organization, or agency, reports to the board of directors. In internal communication and press releases, many companies capitalize the term and those of other high positions, even when they are not proper nouns.
   a. Financial analyst
   b. Chief executive officer
   c. Purchasing manager
   d. Chief brand officer

8. A _____ occurs when an individual or organization (such as a policeman, lawyer, insurance adjuster, politician, engineer, executive, director of a corporation, medical research scientist, physician, writer, editor, or any other entrusted individual or organization) has an interest that might compromise their actions. The presence of a _____ is independent from the execution of impropriety.

In the legal profession, the duty of loyalty owed to a client prohibits an attorney (or a law firm) from representing any other party with interests adverse to those of a current client.

   a. 1990 Clean Air Act
   b. Global Corruption Report
   c. Conflict of interest
   d. 28-hour day

9. _____ is the set of processes, customs, policies, laws, and institutions affecting the way a corporation (or company) is directed, administered or controlled. _____ also includes the relationships among the many stakeholders involved and the goals for which the corporation is governed. The principal stakeholders are the shareholders/members, management, and the board of directors.
   a. Guarantee
   b. Flextime
   c. No-FEAR Act
   d. Corporate governance

10. While _____ literally refers to a person responsible for the performance of duties involved in running an organization, the exact meaning of the role is variable, depending on the organization.

Chapter 3. Organizational Resources and Competitive Advantage

While there is no clear line between executive or principal and inferior officers, principal officers are high-level officials in the executive branch of U.S. government such as department heads of independent agencies. In Humphrey's Executor v. United States, 295 U.S. 602 (1935), the Court distinguished between _____s and quasi-legislative or quasi-judicial officers by stating that the former serve at the pleasure of the President and may be removed at his discretion.

   a. Executive officer
   b. Australian Fair Pay and Conditions Standard
   c. Easement
   d. Unreported employment

11. A _____ is directly responsible for managing the day-to-day operations (and profitability) of a company.

Chief Executive Officer (CEO)
   - As the top manager, the CEO is typically responsible for the entire operations of the corporation and reports directly to the chairman and board of directors. It is the CEO's responsibility to implement board decisions and initiatives and to maintain the smooth operation of the firm, with the assistance of senior management.

   a. Vorstand
   b. Field service management
   c. Getting Things Done
   d. Management team

12. A mutual _____ or stockholder is an individual or company (including a corporation) that legally owns one or more shares of stock in a joint stock company. A company's _____s collectively own that company. Thus, the typical goal of such companies is to enhance _____ value.
   a. Shareholder
   b. 1990 Clean Air Act
   c. Stockholder
   d. Free riding

13. A _____ is a relatively new executive level position at a corporation, company, organization typically reporting directly to the CEO or board of directors. The _____ is responsible for a brand's image, experience, and promise, and propagating it throughout all aspects of the company. The brand officer oversees marketing, advertising, design, public relations and customer service departments.

Chapter 3. Organizational Resources and Competitive Advantage 19

   a. Chief executive officer
   b. Purchasing manager
   c. Chief brand officer
   d. Director of communications

14. _____ is a concept in ethics with several meanings. It is often used synonymously with such concepts as responsibility, answerability, enforcement, blameworthiness, liability and other terms associated with the expectation of account-giving. As an aspect of governance, it has been central to discussions related to problems in both the public and private (corporation) worlds.
   a. Usury
   b. A4e
   c. A Stake in the Outcome
   d. Accountability

15. The _____ of 2002 (Pub.L. 107-204, 116 Stat. 745, enacted July 30, 2002), also known as the Public Company Accounting Reform and Investor Protection Act of 2002 and commonly called Sarbanes-Oxley, Sarbox or SOX, is a United States federal law enacted on July 30, 2002, as a reaction to a number of major corporate and accounting scandals including those affecting Enron, Tyco International, Adelphia, Peregrine Systems and WorldCom.
   a. Fair Labor Standards Act
   b. Letter of credit
   c. Sarbanes-Oxley Act of 2002
   d. Sarbanes-Oxley Act

16. The _____, also known as the Public Company Accounting Reform and Investor Protection Act of 2002 and commonly called Sarbanes-Oxley, Sarbox or SOX, is a United States federal law enacted on July 30, 2002, as a reaction to a number of major corporate and accounting scandals including those affecting Enron, Tyco International, Adelphia, Peregrine Systems and WorldCom.
   a. Sarbanes-Oxley Act of 2002
   b. MacPherson v. Buick Motor Co.
   c. Munn v. Illinois
   d. Letter of credit

17. _____ refers to an assessment of the viability, stability and profitability of a business, sub-business or project.

It is performed by professionals who prepare reports using ratios that make use of information taken from financial statements and other reports. These reports are usually presented to top management as one of their bases in making business decisions.

Chapter 3. Organizational Resources and Competitive Advantage

a. 28-hour day
b. 33 Strategies of War
c. Financial analysis
d. 1990 Clean Air Act

18. _____ is an area of knowledge within organizational theory that studies models and theories about the way an organization learns and adapts.

In Organizational development (OD), learning is a characteristic of an adaptive organization, i.e., an organization that is able to sense changes in signals from its environment (both internal and external) and adapt accordingly.

a. AAAI
b. A Stake in the Outcome
c. A4e
d. Organizational learning

19. _____ is one of a series of accounting transactions dealing with the billing of customers who owe money to a person, company or organization for goods and services that have been provided to the customer. In most business entities this is typically done by generating an invoice and mailing or electronically delivering it to the customer, who in turn must pay it within an established timeframe called credit or payment terms.

An example of a common payment term is Net 30, meaning payment is due in the amount of the invoice 30 days from the date of invoice.

a. Accounts receivable
b. Accumulated Depreciation
c. A Stake in the Outcome
d. Other revenue

20. In business and accounting, _____s are everything of value that is owned by a person or company. Any property or object of value that one possesses, usually considered as applicable to the payment of one's debts is considered an _____. Simplistically stated, _____s are things of value that can be readily converted into cash.

a. AAAI
b. A Stake in the Outcome
c. Asset
d. A4e

21. _____ is a financial ratio that measures the efficiency of a company's use of its assets in generating sales revenue or sales income to the company.

$$Asset\ Turnover = \frac{Sales}{Average\ Total\ Assets}$$

- 'Sales' is the value of 'Net Sales' or 'Sales' from the company's income statement
- 'Average Total Assets' is the value of 'Total assets' from the company's balance sheet in the beginning and the end of the fiscal period divided by 2.

a. A4e
b. A Stake in the Outcome
c. Inventory turnover
d. Asset turnover

22. The _____ is a financial ratio that measures whether or not a firm has enough resources to pay its debts over the next 12 months. It compares a firm's current assets to its current liabilities. It is expressed as follows:

$$Current\ ratio = \frac{Current\ Assets}{Current\ Liabilities}$$

For example, if WXY Company's current assets are $50,000,000 and its current liabilities are $40,000,000, then its _____ would be $50,000,000 divided by $40,000,000, which equals 1.25.

a. Times interest earned
b. Return on assets
c. Financial ratio
d. Current ratio

23. _____ is a financial ratio that indicates the percentage of a company's assets are provided via debt. It is the ratio of total debt (the sum of current liabilities and long-term liabilities) and total assets (the sum of current assets, fixed assets, and other assets such as 'goodwill'.)

$$Debt\ ratio = \frac{Total\ Debt}{Total\ Assets}$$

or alternatively:

Chapter 3. Organizational Resources and Competitive Advantage

$$\text{Debt ratio} = \frac{\text{Total Liability}}{\text{Total Assets}}$$

For example, a company with $2 million in total assets and $500,000 in total liabilities would have a _____ of 25%

Like all financial ratios, a company's _____ should be compared with their industry average or other competing firms.

a. 28-hour day
b. Demand forecasting
c. 1990 Clean Air Act
d. Debt ratio

24. In finance, a _____ or accounting ratio is a ratio of two selected numerical values taken from an enterprise's financial statements. There are many standard ratios used to try to evaluate the overall financial condition of a corporation or other organization. _____s may be used by managers within a firm, by current and potential shareholders (owners) of a firm, and by a firm's creditors.
   a. Return on equity
   b. Return on sales
   c. Rate of return
   d. Financial ratio

25. In accounting, _____ or sales profit is the difference between revenue and the cost of making a product or providing a service, before deducting overhead, payroll, taxation, and interest payments. Note that this is different from operating profit (earnings before interest and taxes.)

Net sales are calculated:

    Net sales = Sales - Sales returns and allowances.

a. Gross profit
b. Gross profit margin
c. Cash flow
d. Capital budgeting

26. _____ is a financial ratio used to assess the profitability of a firm's core activities, excluding fixed costs.

Chapter 3. Organizational Resources and Competitive Advantage

The general calculation is:

> [formula]

The _____ is related to the net profit margin, which assesses the profitability of an organization after including fixed costs.

_____ indicates the relationship between net sales revenue and the cost of goods sold.

a. Shareholder value
b. Capital structure
c. Sweat equity
d. Gross profit margin

27. The _____ is an equation that equals the cost of goods sold divided by the average inventory. Average inventory equals beginning inventory plus ending inventory divided by 2.

The formula for _____:

> [formula]

The formula for average inventory:

> [formula]

A low turnover rate may point to overstocking, obsolescence, or deficiencies in the product line or marketing effort.

a. A Stake in the Outcome
b. Asset turnover
c. A4e
d. Inventory turnover

28. In finance, _____ is borrowing money to supplement existing funds for investment in such a way that the potential positive or negative outcome is magnified and/or enhanced. It generally refers to using borrowed funds, or debt, so as to attempt to increase the returns to equity. Deleveraging is the action of reducing borrowings.

Chapter 3. Organizational Resources and Competitive Advantage

   a. Limited partners
   b. Private equity
   c. Limited liability corporation
   d. Gearing

29. Market _____ is a business, economics or investment term that refers to an asset's ability to be easily converted through an act of buying or selling without causing a significant movement in the price and with minimum loss of value. Money, or cash on hand, is the most liquid asset. An act of exchange of a less liquid asset with a more liquid asset is called liquidation.
   a. 33 Strategies of War
   b. 28-hour day
   c. Liquidity
   d. 1990 Clean Air Act

30. In business and finance accounting, _____ is equal to the gross profit minus overheads minus interest payable plus/minus one off items for a given time period (usually: accounting period.)

A common synonym for '_____' when discussing financial statements (which include a balance sheet and an income statement) is the bottom line. This term results from the traditional appearance of an income statement which shows all allocated revenues and expenses over a specified time period with the resulting summation on the bottom line of the report.

   a. Net profit
   b. Treasury stock
   c. Matching principle
   d. Generally accepted accounting principles

31. Profit margin, net margin, _____ or net profit ratio all refer to a measure of profitability. It is calculated by finding the net profit as a percentage of the revenue.

The profit margin is mostly used for internal comparison.

Chapter 3. Organizational Resources and Competitive Advantage

a. Profit maximization
b. Profit margin
c. 1990 Clean Air Act
d. Net profit margin

32. _____, net margin, net _____ or net profit ratio all refer to a measure of profitability. It is calculated by finding the net profit as a percentage of the revenue.

$$\text{Net profit margin} = \frac{\text{Net profit (after taxes)}}{\text{Revenue}} \times 100\%$$

The _____ is mostly used for internal comparison.

a. Profit margin
b. 1990 Clean Air Act
c. Profit maximization
d. Net profit margin

33. In finance, the _____ or quick ratio or liquid ratio measures the ability of a company to use its near cash or quick assets to immediately extinguish or retire its current liabilities. Quick assets include those current assets that presumably can be quickly converted to cash at close to their book values.

Generally, the acid test ratio should be 1:1 or better, however this varies widely by industry.

a. Inventory turnover
b. A Stake in the Outcome
c. A4e
d. Acid-test

34. In a human resources context, _____ or labor _____ is the rate at which an employer gains and loses employees. Simple ways to describe it are 'how long employees tend to stay' or 'the rate of traffic through the revolving door.' _____ is measured for individual companies and for their industry as a whole. If an employer is said to have a high _____ relative to its competitors, it means that employees of that company have a shorter average tenure than those of other companies in the same industry.

Chapter 3. Organizational Resources and Competitive Advantage

a. Career portfolios
b. Continuous
c. Turnover
d. Ten year occupational employment projection

35. _____ is a strategic planning method used to evaluate the Strengths, Weaknesses, Opportunities, and Threats involved in a project or in a business venture. It involves specifying the objective of the business venture or project and identifying the internal and external factors that are favorable and unfavorable to achieving that objective. The technique is credited to Albert Humphrey, who led a convention at Stanford University in the 1960s and 1970s using data from Fortune 500 companies.

a. Corporate image
b. Market share
c. SWOT analysis
d. Marketing

36. The _____ is a chart that had been created by Bruce Henderson for the Boston Consulting Group in 1970 to help corporations with analyzing their business units or product lines. This helps the company allocate resources and is used as an analytical tool in brand marketing, product management, strategic management, and portfolio analysis. _____

To use the chart, analysts plot a scatter graph to rank the business units (or products) on the basis of their relative market shares and growth rates.

a. Market segment
b. Marketing strategy
c. Marketing plan
d. BCG matrix

37. A _____ is a name or trademark connected with a product or producer. _____s have become increasingly important components of culture and the economy, now being described as 'cultural accessories and personal philosophies'.

Some people distinguish the psychological aspect of a _____ from the experiential aspect.

a. Brand awareness
b. Brand loyalty
c. Brand extension
d. Brand

Chapter 3. Organizational Resources and Competitive Advantage

38. In general, a _____ is an arrangement to provide people with an income when they are no longer earning a regular income from employment.

The terms retirement plan or superannuation refer to a _____ granted upon retirement. Retirement plans may be set up by employers, insurance companies, the government or other institutions such as employer associations or trade unions.

   a. Pension
   b. State Compensation Insurance Fund
   c. Wage
   d. Pension insurance contract

39. _____ is the management of the flow of goods, information and other resources, including energy and people, between the point of origin and the point of consumption in order to meet the requirements of consumers (frequently, and originally, military organizations.) _____ involves the integration of information, transportation, inventory, warehousing, material-handling, and packaging, and occasionally security. _____ is a channel of the supply chain which adds the value of time and place utility.
   a. Logistics
   b. Third-party logistics
   c. 28-hour day
   d. 1990 Clean Air Act

40. _____ is an integrated communications-based process through which individuals and communities discover that existing and newly-identified needs and wants may be satisfied by the products and services of others.

_____ is defined by the American _____ Association as the activity, set of institutions, and processes for creating, communicating, delivering, and exchanging offerings that have value for customers, clients, partners, and society at large. The term developed from the original meaning which referred literally to going to market, as in shopping, or going to a market to buy or sell goods or services.

   a. Marketing
   b. Market development
   c. Customer relationship management
   d. Disruptive technology

41. _____ is the acquisition of goods and/or services at the best possible total cost of ownership, in the right quality and quantity, at the right time, in the right place and from the right source for the direct benefit or use of corporations, individuals generally via a contract. Simple _____ may involve nothing more than repeat purchasing. Complex _____ could involve finding long term partners - or even 'co-destiny' suppliers that might fundamentally commit one organization to another.

a. Psychological pricing
b. Sole proprietorship
c. Procurement
d. Golden parachute

42. _____ is an advertisement in which a particular product specifically mentions a competitor by name for the express purpose of showing why the competitor is inferior to the product naming it.

This should not be confused with parody advertisements, where a fictional product is being advertised for the purpose of poking fun at the particular advertisement, nor should it be confused with the use of a coined brand name for the purpose of comparing the product without actually naming an actual competitor. ('Wikipedia tastes better and is less filling than the Encyclopedia Galactica.')

In the 1980s, during what has been referred to as the cola wars, soft-drink manufacturer Pepsi ran a series of advertisements where people, caught on hidden camera, in a blind taste test, chose Pepsi over rival Coca-Cola.

a. 28-hour day
b. 1990 Clean Air Act
c. 33 Strategies of War
d. Comparative advertising

43. The _____ is a concept from business management that was first described and popularized by Michael Porter in his 1985 best-seller, Competitive Advantage: Creating and Sustaining Superior Performance.

A _____ is a chain of activities. Products pass through all activities of the chain in order and at each activity the product gains some value. The chain of activities gives the products more added value than the sum of added values of all activities. It is important not to mix the concept of the _____ with the costs occurring throughout the activities.

a. Market development
b. Customer relationship management
c. Mass marketing
d. Value chain

Chapter 4. Strategic Direction

1. _____ is an organization's process of defining its strategy and making decisions on allocating its resources to pursue this strategy, including its capital and people. Various business analysis techniques can be used in _____, including SWOT analysis (Strengths, Weaknesses, Opportunities, and Threats) and PEST analysis (Political, Economic, Social, and Technological analysis) or STEER analysis involving Socio-cultural, Technological, Economic, Ecological, and Regulatory factors and EPISTEL (Environment, Political, Informatic, Social, Technological, Economic and Legal)

_____ is the formal consideration of an organization's future course. All _____ deals with at least one of three key questions:

1. 'What do we do?'
2. 'For whom do we do it?'
3. 'How do we excel?'

In business _____, the third question is better phrased 'How can we beat or avoid competition?'. (Bradford and Duncan, page 1.)

a. 1990 Clean Air Act
b. 28-hour day
c. 33 Strategies of War
d. Strategic planning

2. A _____ is a brief written statement of the purpose of a company or organization. Ideally, a _____ guides the actions of the organization, spells out its overall goal, provides a sense of direction, and guides decision making for all levels of management.

_____s often contain the following:

- Purpose and aim of the organization
- The organization's primary stakeholders: clients, stockholders, etc.
- Responsibilities of the organization toward these stakeholders
- Products and services offered

In developing a _____:

- Encourage as much input as feasible from employees, volunteers, and other stakeholders
- Publicize it broadly

The _____ can be used to resolve differences between business stakeholders. Stakeholders include: employees including managers and executives, stockholders, board of directors, customers, suppliers, distributors, creditors, governments (local, state, federal, etc.), unions, competitors, NGO's, and the general public.

a. 28-hour day
b. 1990 Clean Air Act
c. 33 Strategies of War
d. Mission statement

3. A _____ is the system of organizations, people, technology, activities, information and resources involved in moving a product or service from supplier to customer. _____ activities transform natural resources, raw materials and components into a finished product that is delivered to the end customer. In sophisticated _____ systems, used products may re-enter the _____ at any point where residual value is recyclable.
   a. Wholesalers
   b. Packaging
   c. Drop shipping
   d. Supply chain

4. In microeconomics and management, the term _____ describes a style of management control. Vertically integrated companies are united through a hierarchy with a common owner. Usually each member of the hierarchy produces a different product or (market-specific) service, and the products combine to satisfy a common need.
   a. 1990 Clean Air Act
   b. Vertical integration
   c. 28-hour day
   d. 33 Strategies of War

5. _____ is the ethics of an organization, and it is how an organization ethically responds to an internal or external stimulus. _____ is interdependent with the organizational culture. Although, it is akin to both organizational behavior (OB) and business ethics on the micro and macro levels, _____ is neither OB, nor is it solely business ethics (which includes corporate governance and corporate ethics.)
   a. AAAI
   b. A Stake in the Outcome
   c. A4e
   d. Organizational ethics

6. An _____ is a situation that will often involve an apparent conflict between moral imperatives, in which to obey one would result in transgressing another. This is also called an ethical paradox since in moral philosophy, paradox plays a central role in ethics debates. For instance, an ethical admonition to 'love thy neighbour as thy self' is not always just in contrast with, but sometimes in contradiction to an armed neighbour actively trying to kill you: if he or she succeeds, you will not be able to love him or her.

a. AAAI
b. A4e
c. A Stake in the Outcome
d. Ethical dilemma

7. _____ is a form of corporate self-regulation integrated into a business model. Ideally, _____ policy would function as a built-in, self-regulating mechanism whereby business would monitor and ensure their adherence to law, ethical standards, and international norms. Business would embrace responsibility for the impact of their activities on the environment, consumers, employees, communities, stakeholders and all other members of the public sphere.

a. 1990 Clean Air Act
b. 33 Strategies of War
c. Corporate social responsibility
d. 28-hour day

8. _____ is a concept in ethics with several meanings. It is often used synonymously with such concepts as responsibility, answerability, enforcement, blameworthiness, liability and other terms associated with the expectation of account-giving. As an aspect of governance, it has been central to discussions related to problems in both the public and private (corporation) worlds.

a. Accountability
b. A Stake in the Outcome
c. A4e
d. Usury

9. A _____ is a name or trademark connected with a product or producer. _____s have become increasingly important components of culture and the economy, now being described as 'cultural accessories and personal philosophies'.

Some people distinguish the psychological aspect of a _____ from the experiential aspect.

a. Brand extension
b. Brand loyalty
c. Brand awareness
d. Brand

10. _____ is a pattern of resource use that aims to meet human needs while preserving the environment so that these needs can be met not only in the present, but also for future generations. The term was used by the Brundtland Commission which coined what has become the most often-quoted definition of _____ as development that 'meets the needs of the present without compromising the ability of future generations to meet their own needs.'

_____ ties together concern for the carrying capacity of natural systems with the social challenges facing humanity. As early as the 1970s 'sustainability' was employed to describe an economy 'in equilibrium with basic ecological support systems.' Ecologists have pointed to the 'limits of growth' and presented the alternative of a 'steady state economy' in order to address environmental concerns.

a. Global Reporting Initiative
b. Sustainable development
c. Sustainable business
d. Sustainability reporting

Chapter 5. Business-Level Strategies

1. _____ is, in very basic words, a position a firm occupies against its competitors.

According to Michael Porter, the three methods for creating a sustainable _____ are through:

1. Cost leadership

2. Differentiation

3. Focus (economics)

   a. 28-hour day
   b. Competitive Advantage
   c. Theory Z
   d. 1990 Clean Air Act

2. A _____ strategy targets non-buying customers in currently targeted segments. It also targets new customers in new segments. (Winer)

A marketing manager has to think about the following questions before implementing a _____ strategy: Is it profitable? Will it require the introduction of new or modified products? Is the customer and channel well enough researched and understood?

The marketing manager uses these four groups to give more focus to the market segment decision: existing customers, competitor customers, non-buying in current segments, new segments.

   a. Customer relationship management
   b. Context analysis
   c. Market development
   d. Product line

3. _____ is one of the four growth strategies of the Product-Market Growth Matrix defined by Ansoff. _____ occurs when a company enters/penetrates a market with current products. The best way to achieve this is by gaining competitors' customers (part of their market share.)
   a. Market penetration
   b. 1990 Clean Air Act
   c. 33 Strategies of War
   d. 28-hour day

Chapter 5. Business-Level Strategies

4. In business and engineering, new _____ is the term used to describe the complete process of bringing a new product or service to market. There are two parallel paths involved in the NProduct development process: one involves the idea generation, product design, and detail engineering; the other involves market research and marketing analysis. Companies typically see new _____ as the first stage in generating and commercializing new products within the overall strategic process of product life cycle management used to maintain or grow their market share.

   a. 28-hour day
   b. 33 Strategies of War
   c. 1990 Clean Air Act
   d. Product development

5. _____ is an advertisement in which a particular product specifically mentions a competitor by name for the express purpose of showing why the competitor is inferior to the product naming it.

This should not be confused with parody advertisements, where a fictional product is being advertised for the purpose of poking fun at the particular advertisement, nor should it be confused with the use of a coined brand name for the purpose of comparing the product without actually naming an actual competitor. ('Wikipedia tastes better and is less filling than the Encyclopedia Galactica.')

In the 1980s, during what has been referred to as the cola wars, soft-drink manufacturer Pepsi ran a series of advertisements where people, caught on hidden camera, in a blind taste test, chose Pepsi over rival Coca-Cola.

   a. Comparative advertising
   b. 1990 Clean Air Act
   c. 28-hour day
   d. 33 Strategies of War

6. The phrase mergers and _____s refers to the aspect of corporate strategy, corporate finance and management dealing with the buying, selling and combining of different companies that can aid, finance, or help a growing company in a given industry grow rapidly without having to create another business entity.

An _____, also known as a takeover or a buyout, is the buying of one company (the 'target') by another. An _____ may be friendly or hostile.

   a. AAAI
   b. A Stake in the Outcome
   c. Acquisition
   d. A4e

Chapter 5. Business-Level Strategies

7. In microeconomics and strategic management, the term _____ describes a type of ownership and control. It is a strategy used by a business or corporation that seeks to sell a type of product in numerous markets. _____ in marketing is much more common than vertical integration is in production.
   a. Career development
   b. Farmshoring
   c. No-bid contract
   d. Horizontal integration

8. A _____ is a relatively new executive level position at a corporation, company, organization typically reporting directly to the CEO or board of directors. The _____ is responsible for a brand's image, experience, and promise, and propagating it throughout all aspects of the company. The brand officer oversees marketing, advertising, design, public relations and customer service departments.
   a. Chief executive officer
   b. Director of communications
   c. Purchasing manager
   d. Chief brand officer

9. In economics, _____ are obstacles in the path of a firm which wants to leave a given market or industrial sector. These obstacles often cost the firm financially to leave the market and may prohibit it doing so.

If the barriers of exit are significant; a firm may be forced to continue competing in a market, as the costs of leaving may be higher than those incurred if they continue competing in the market.

   a. Barriers to exit
   b. 1990 Clean Air Act
   c. 33 Strategies of War
   d. 28-hour day

10. A _____ is an entity formed between two or more parties to undertake economic activity together. The parties agree to create a new entity by both contributing equity, and they then share in the revenues, expenses, and control of the enterprise. The venture can be for one specific project only, or a continuing business relationship such as the Fuji Xerox _____.
    a. Patent
    b. Joint venture
    c. Meritor Savings Bank v. Vinson
    d. Civil Rights Act of 1991

Chapter 5. Business-Level Strategies

11. A _____ is a formal relationship between two or more parties to pursue a set of agreed upon goals or to meet a critical business need while remaining independent organizations.

Partners may provide the _____ with resources such as products, distribution channels, manufacturing capability, project funding, capital equipment, knowledge, expertise, or intellectual property. The alliance is a cooperation or collaboration which aims for a synergy where each partner hopes that the benefits from the alliance will be greater than those from individual efforts.

   a. Strategic alliance
   b. Golden parachute
   c. Farmshoring
   d. Process automation

12. An _____ is a person who has possession of an enterprise and assumes significant accountability for the inherent risks and the outcome. It is an ambitious leader who combines land, labor, and capital to create and market new goods or services. The term is a loanword from French and was first defined by the Irish economist Richard Cantillon.
   a. A Stake in the Outcome
   b. AAAI
   c. A4e
   d. Entrepreneur

13. _____ is a legally declared inability or impairment of ability of an individual or organization to pay its creditors. Creditors may file a _____ petition against a debtor ('involuntary _____') in an effort to recoup a portion of what they are owed or initiate a restructuring. In the majority of cases, however, _____ is initiated by the debtor (a 'voluntary _____' that is filed by the insolvent individual or organization.)
   a. 28-hour day
   b. 1990 Clean Air Act
   c. 33 Strategies of War
   d. Bankruptcy

14. _____ is the advantage gained by the initial occupant of a market segment. This advantage may stem from the fact that the first entrant can gain control of resources that followers may not be able to match. Sometimes the first mover is not able to capitalise on its advantage, leaving the opportunity for another firm to gain second-mover advantage.
   a. Customer retention
   b. First-mover advantage
   c. Horizontal integration
   d. Business ecosystem

Chapter 5. Business-Level Strategies

15. The _____ of 2002 (Pub.L. 107-204, 116 Stat. 745, enacted July 30, 2002), also known as the Public Company Accounting Reform and Investor Protection Act of 2002 and commonly called Sarbanes-Oxley, Sarbox or SOX, is a United States federal law enacted on July 30, 2002, as a reaction to a number of major corporate and accounting scandals including those affecting Enron, Tyco International, Adelphia, Peregrine Systems and WorldCom.
   a. Fair Labor Standards Act
   b. Letter of credit
   c. Sarbanes-Oxley Act of 2002
   d. Sarbanes-Oxley Act

16. The _____, also known as the Public Company Accounting Reform and Investor Protection Act of 2002 and commonly called Sarbanes-Oxley, Sarbox or SOX, is a United States federal law enacted on July 30, 2002, as a reaction to a number of major corporate and accounting scandals including those affecting Enron, Tyco International, Adelphia, Peregrine Systems and WorldCom.
   a. MacPherson v. Buick Motor Co.
   b. Munn v. Illinois
   c. Letter of credit
   d. Sarbanes-Oxley Act of 2002

17. _____ is a concept in economics which refers to the extent to which an enterprise or a nation actually uses its installed productive capacity. Thus, it refers to the relationship between actual output that 'is' produced with the installed equipment and the potential output which 'could' be produced with it, if capacity was fully used.

    If market demand grows, _____ will rise.

   a. Multifactor productivity
   b. Factors of production
   c. Diseconomies of scale
   d. Capacity utilization

18. In economics, business, retail, and accounting, a _____ is the value of money that has been used up to produce something, and hence is not available for use anymore. In economics, a _____ is an alternative that is given up as a result of a decision. In business, the _____ may be one of acquisition, in which case the amount of money expended to acquire it is counted as _____.
   a. Cost allocation
   b. Fixed costs
   c. Cost overrun
   d. Cost

Chapter 5. Business-Level Strategies

19. _____ is a concept developed by Michael Porter, used in business strategy. It describes a way to establish the competitive advantage. _____, in basic words, means the lowest cost of operation in the industry.

   a. Switching cost
   b. Strategic business unit
   c. Strategic group
   d. Cost leadership

20. _____ has been described as the 'process of social influence in which one person can enlist the aid and support of others in the accomplishment of a common task'. A definition more inclusive of followers comes from Alan Keith of Genentech who said '_____ is ultimately about creating a way for people to contribute to making something extraordinary happen.'

_____ is one of the most salient aspects of the organizational context. However, defining _____ has been challenging.

   a. 1990 Clean Air Act
   b. Situational leadership
   c. 28-hour day
   d. Leadership

21. Network externalities resemble economies of scale, but they are not considered such because they are a function of the number of users of a good or service in an industry, not of the production efficiency within a business. _____ are only considered examples of network externalities if they are driven by demand side economies.

Formally, a production function ⟨×⟩ is defined to have:

- constant returns to scale if (for any constant a greater than or equal to 0) ⟨×⟩
- increasing returns to scale if (for any constant a greater than 1) ⟨×⟩
- decreasing returns to scale if (for any constant a greater than 1) ⟨×⟩

where K and L are factors of production, capital and labour, respectively.

As an example, the Cobb-Douglas functional form has constant returns to scale when the sum of the exponents adds up to one.

a. A4e
b. A Stake in the Outcome
c. AAAI
d. Economies of scale external to the firm

22. In queueing theory, _____ is the proportion of the system's resources which is used by the traffic which arrives at it. It should be strictly less than one for the system to function well. It is usually represented by the symbol ρ.
    a. A Stake in the Outcome
    b. AAAI
    c. A4e
    d. Utilization

23. The United Nations _____ is an United Nations initiative to encourage businesses worldwide to adopt sustainable and socially responsible policies, and to report on their implementation. The _____ is a principle based framework for businesses, stating ten principles in the areas of human rights, labour, the environment and anti-corruption. Under the _____, companies are brought together with UN agencies, labour groups and civil society.
    a. Global Compact
    b. 28-hour day
    c. 33 Strategies of War
    d. 1990 Clean Air Act

24. _____ is exchange of capital, goods, and services across international borders or territories. In most countries, it represents a significant share of gross domestic product (GDP.) While _____ has been present throughout much of history, its economic, social, and political importance has been on the rise in recent centuries.
    a. AAAI
    b. A Stake in the Outcome
    c. A4e
    d. International trade

25. _____ refers to the methods of practicing and using another person's business philosophy. The franchisor grants the independent operator the right to distribute its products, techniques, and trademarks for a percentage of gross monthly sales and a royalty fee. Various tangibles and intangibles such as national or international advertising, training, and other support services are commonly made available by the franchisor.

a. 28-hour day
b. 1990 Clean Air Act
c. ServiceMaster
d. Franchising

26. A _____ or transnational corporation is a corporation or enterprise that manages production or delivers services in more than one country. It can also be referred to as an international corporation.

The first modern _____ is generally thought to be the Dutch East India Company, established in 1602.

a. Command center
b. Small and medium enterprises
c. Financial Accounting Standards Board
d. Multinational corporation

27. A _____ is something for which there is demand, but which is supplied without qualitative differentiation across a market. It is a product that is the same no matter who produces it, such as petroleum, notebook paper, or milk. In other words, copper is copper.
a. 28-hour day
b. 1990 Clean Air Act
c. 33 Strategies of War
d. Commodity

28. _____ Management is the succession of strategies used by management as a product goes through its _____. The conditions in which a product is sold changes over time and must be managed as it moves through its succession of stages.

The _____ goes through many phases, involves many professional disciplines, and requires many skills, tools and processes.

a. Golden handshake
b. Strategic Alliance
c. Product life cycle
d. Job hunting

Chapter 6. Corporate Strategies

41

1. _____ is, in very basic words, a position a firm occupies against its competitors.

According to Michael Porter, the three methods for creating a sustainable _____ are through:

1. Cost leadership

2. Differentiation

3. Focus (economics)

   a. Competitive Advantage
   b. 1990 Clean Air Act
   c. Theory Z
   d. 28-hour day

2. _____ is a legally declared inability or impairment of ability of an individual or organization to pay its creditors. Creditors may file a _____ petition against a debtor ('involuntary _____') in an effort to recoup a portion of what they are owed or initiate a restructuring. In the majority of cases, however, _____ is initiated by the debtor (a 'voluntary _____' that is filed by the insolvent individual or organization.)
   a. 28-hour day
   b. Bankruptcy
   c. 33 Strategies of War
   d. 1990 Clean Air Act

3. A _____ is the system of organizations, people, technology, activities, information and resources involved in moving a product or service from supplier to customer. _____ activities transform natural resources, raw materials and components into a finished product that is delivered to the end customer. In sophisticated _____ systems, used products may re-enter the _____ at any point where residual value is recyclable.
   a. Wholesalers
   b. Supply chain
   c. Drop shipping
   d. Packaging

4. In microeconomics and management, the term _____ describes a style of management control. Vertically integrated companies are united through a hierarchy with a common owner. Usually each member of the hierarchy produces a different product or (market-specific) service, and the products combine to satisfy a common need.

a. Vertical integration
b. 28-hour day
c. 1990 Clean Air Act
d. 33 Strategies of War

5. In economics, business, retail, and accounting, a _____ is the value of money that has been used up to produce something, and hence is not available for use anymore. In economics, a _____ is an alternative that is given up as a result of a decision. In business, the _____ may be one of acquisition, in which case the amount of money expended to acquire it is counted as _____.
   a. Cost overrun
   b. Cost allocation
   c. Cost
   d. Fixed costs

6. In economics and related disciplines, a _____ is a cost incurred in making an economic exchange. For example, most people, when buying or selling a stock, must pay a commission to their broker; that commission is a _____ of doing the stock deal. Or consider buying a banana from a store; to purchase the banana, your costs will be not only the price of the banana itself, but also the energy and effort it requires to find out which of the various banana products you prefer, where to get them and at what price, the cost of traveling from your house to the store and back, the time waiting in line, and the effort of the paying itself; the costs above and beyond the cost of the banana are the _____s.
   a. Cost accounting
   b. Cost overrun
   c. Transaction cost
   d. Fixed costs

7. _____ is a strategic planning method used to evaluate the Strengths, Weaknesses, Opportunities, and Threats involved in a project or in a business venture. It involves specifying the objective of the business venture or project and identifying the internal and external factors that are favorable and unfavorable to achieving that objective. The technique is credited to Albert Humphrey, who led a convention at Stanford University in the 1960s and 1970s using data from Fortune 500 companies.
   a. Marketing
   b. SWOT analysis
   c. Market share
   d. Corporate image

8. _____ is the term used to describe a situation where different entities cooperate advantageously for a final outcome. Simply defined, it means that the whole is greater than the sum of the individual parts. Although the whole will be greater than each individual part, this is not the concept of _____.

a. 33 Strategies of War
b. 28-hour day
c. 1990 Clean Air Act
d. Synergy

9. The phrase mergers and _____s refers to the aspect of corporate strategy, corporate finance and management dealing with the buying, selling and combining of different companies that can aid, finance, or help a growing company in a given industry grow rapidly without having to create another business entity.

An _____, also known as a takeover or a buyout, is the buying of one company (the 'target') by another. An _____ may be friendly or hostile.

a. AAAI
b. A Stake in the Outcome
c. Acquisition
d. A4e

10. An _____ is a person who has possession of an enterprise and assumes significant accountability for the inherent risks and the outcome. It is an ambitious leader who combines land, labor, and capital to create and market new goods or services. The term is a loanword from French and was first defined by the Irish economist Richard Cantillon.
a. A4e
b. AAAI
c. A Stake in the Outcome
d. Entrepreneur

11. The United Nations _____ is an United Nations initiative to encourage businesses worldwide to adopt sustainable and socially responsible policies, and to report on their implementation. The _____ is a principle based framework for businesses, stating ten principles in the areas of human rights, labour, the environment and anti-corruption. Under the _____, companies are brought together with UN agencies, labour groups and civil society.
a. Global Compact
b. 28-hour day
c. 1990 Clean Air Act
d. 33 Strategies of War

12. A _____ is an agreement between a company and an employee (usually upper executive) specifying that the employee will receive certain significant benefits if employment is terminated. Sometimes, certain conditions, typically a change in company ownership, must be met, but often the cause of termination is unspecified. These benefits may include severance pay, cash bonuses, stock options, or other benefits.

a. Job hunting
b. Career development
c. Golden parachute
d. First-mover advantage

13. _____ is a term referring to any strategy, generally in business or politics, to increase the likelihood of negative results over positive ones for a party that attempts any kind of takeover. It derives from its original meaning of a literal _____ carried by various spies throughout history, taken when discovered to eliminate the possibility of being interrogated for the enemy's gain.

In publicly held companies, various methods to avoid takeover bids are called '_____s'.

a. 28-hour day
b. 33 Strategies of War
c. 1990 Clean Air Act
d. Poison pill

14. A _____ is an entity formed between two or more parties to undertake economic activity together. The parties agree to create a new entity by both contributing equity, and they then share in the revenues, expenses, and control of the enterprise. The venture can be for one specific project only, or a continuing business relationship such as the Fuji Xerox _____.

a. Joint venture
b. Patent
c. Civil Rights Act of 1991
d. Meritor Savings Bank v. Vinson

15. A _____ is a formal relationship between two or more parties to pursue a set of agreed upon goals or to meet a critical business need while remaining independent organizations.

Partners may provide the _____ with resources such as products, distribution channels, manufacturing capability, project funding, capital equipment, knowledge, expertise, or intellectual property. The alliance is a cooperation or collaboration which aims for a synergy where each partner hopes that the benefits from the alliance will be greater than those from individual efforts.

a. Farmshoring
b. Process automation
c. Golden parachute
d. Strategic alliance

16. The _____ is a chart that had been created by Bruce Henderson for the Boston Consulting Group in 1970 to help corporations with analyzing their business units or product lines. This helps the company allocate resources and is used as an analytical tool in brand marketing, product management, strategic management, and portfolio analysis. _____

To use the chart, analysts plot a scatter graph to rank the business units (or products) on the basis of their relative market shares and growth rates.

a. Marketing strategy
b. Marketing plan
c. Market segment
d. BCG matrix

17. _____, in strategic management and marketing is, according to Carlton O'Neal, the percentage or proportion of the total available market or market segment that is being serviced by a company. It can be expressed as a company's sales revenue (from that market) divided by the total sales revenue available in that market. It can also be expressed as a company's unit sales volume (in a market) divided by the total volume of units sold in that market.

a. Marketing plan
b. Green marketing
c. Business-to-business
d. Market share

Chapter 7. Strategy Implementation

1. _____ has been described as the 'process of social influence in which one person can enlist the aid and support of others in the accomplishment of a common task' . A definition more inclusive of followers comes from Alan Keith of Genentech who said '_____ is ultimately about creating a way for people to contribute to making something extraordinary happen.'

_____ is one of the most salient aspects of the organizational context. However, defining _____ has been challenging.

   a. 1990 Clean Air Act
   b. Situational leadership
   c. Leadership
   d. 28-hour day

2. _____ is a concept in ethics with several meanings. It is often used synonymously with such concepts as responsibility, answerability, enforcement, blameworthiness, liability and other terms associated with the expectation of account-giving. As an aspect of governance, it has been central to discussions related to problems in both the public and private (corporation) worlds.
   a. A Stake in the Outcome
   b. A4e
   c. Usury
   d. Accountability

3. The _____ of 2002 (Pub.L. 107-204, 116 Stat. 745, enacted July 30, 2002), also known as the Public Company Accounting Reform and Investor Protection Act of 2002 and commonly called Sarbanes-Oxley, Sarbox or SOX, is a United States federal law enacted on July 30, 2002, as a reaction to a number of major corporate and accounting scandals including those affecting Enron, Tyco International, Adelphia, Peregrine Systems and WorldCom.
   a. Letter of credit
   b. Sarbanes-Oxley Act
   c. Fair Labor Standards Act
   d. Sarbanes-Oxley Act of 2002

4. The _____, also known as the Public Company Accounting Reform and Investor Protection Act of 2002 and commonly called Sarbanes-Oxley, Sarbox or SOX, is a United States federal law enacted on July 30, 2002, as a reaction to a number of major corporate and accounting scandals including those affecting Enron, Tyco International, Adelphia, Peregrine Systems and WorldCom.
   a. Letter of credit
   b. MacPherson v. Buick Motor Co.
   c. Munn v. Illinois
   d. Sarbanes-Oxley Act of 2002

Chapter 7. Strategy Implementation

5. _____ is an idea in the field of Organizational studies and management which describes the psychology, attitudes, experiences, beliefs and Values (personal and cultural values) of an organization. It has been defined as 'the specific collection of values and norms that are shared by people and groups in an organization and that control the way they interact with each other and with stakeholders outside the organization.'

This definition continues to explain organizational values also known as 'beliefs and ideas about what kinds of goals members of an organization should pursue and ideas about the appropriate kinds or standards of behavior organizational members should use to achieve these goals. From organizational values develop organizational norms, guidelines or expectations that prescribe appropriate kinds of behavior by employees in particular situations and control the behavior of organizational members towards one another.'

_____ is not the same as corporate culture.

   a. Organizational effectiveness
   b. Organizational culture
   c. Organizational development
   d. Union shop

6. _____ is an integrated communications-based process through which individuals and communities discover that existing and newly-identified needs and wants may be satisfied by the products and services of others.

_____ is defined by the American _____ Association as the activity, set of institutions, and processes for creating, communicating, delivering, and exchanging offerings that have value for customers, clients, partners, and society at large. The term developed from the original meaning which referred literally to going to market, as in shopping, or going to a market to buy or sell goods or services.

   a. Customer relationship management
   b. Disruptive technology
   c. Market development
   d. Marketing

7. A _____ is a process that can allow an organization to concentrate its limited resources on the greatest opportunities to increase sales and achieve a sustainable competitive advantage. A _____ should be centered around the key concept that customer satisfaction is the main goal.

A _____ is a written plan which combines product development, promotion, distribution, and pricing approach, identifies the firm's marketing goals, and explains how they will be achieved within a stated timeframe.

a. Product bundling
b. Disruptive technology
c. Category management
d. Marketing strategy

8. The _____ captures an expanded spectrum of values and criteria for measuring organizational success: economic, ecological and social. With the ratification of the United Nations and ICLEI _____ standard for urban and community accounting in early 2007, this became the dominant approach to public sector full cost accounting. Similar UN standards apply to natural capital and human capital measurement to assist in measurements required by _____, e.g. the ecoBudget standard for reporting ecological footprint.
   a. 33 Strategies of War
   b. 28-hour day
   c. 1990 Clean Air Act
   d. Triple bottom line

9. In general, a _____ is an arrangement to provide people with an income when they are no longer earning a regular income from employment.

The terms retirement plan or superannuation refer to a _____ granted upon retirement. Retirement plans may be set up by employers, insurance companies, the government or other institutions such as employer associations or trade unions.

   a. Wage
   b. Pension
   c. State Compensation Insurance Fund
   d. Pension insurance contract

10. The phrase _____, according to the Organization for Economic Co-operation and Development, refers to 'creative work undertaken on a systematic basis in order to increase the stock of knowledge, including knowledge of man, culture and society, and the use of this stock of knowledge to devise new applications [sic]'

New product design and development is more than often a crucial factor in the survival of a company. In an industry that is fast changing, firms must continually revise their design and range of products. This is necessary due to continuous technology change and development as well as other competitors and the changing preference of customers.

a. 28-hour day
b. 1990 Clean Air Act
c. Research and development
d. 33 Strategies of War

11. _____ is, in very basic words, a position a firm occupies against its competitors.

According to Michael Porter, the three methods for creating a sustainable _____ are through:

1. Cost leadership

2. Differentiation

3. Focus (economics)

   a. Theory Z
   b. 28-hour day
   c. 1990 Clean Air Act
   d. Competitive Advantage

12. _____ is an advertisement in which a particular product specifically mentions a competitor by name for the express purpose of showing why the competitor is inferior to the product naming it.

This should not be confused with parody advertisements, where a fictional product is being advertised for the purpose of poking fun at the particular advertisement, nor should it be confused with the use of a coined brand name for the purpose of comparing the product without actually naming an actual competitor. ('Wikipedia tastes better and is less filling than the Encyclopedia Galactica.')

In the 1980s, during what has been referred to as the cola wars, soft-drink manufacturer Pepsi ran a series of advertisements where people, caught on hidden camera, in a blind taste test, chose Pepsi over rival Coca-Cola.

   a. 1990 Clean Air Act
   b. 33 Strategies of War
   c. 28-hour day
   d. Comparative advertising

13. _____ is an increasingly broadening term with which an organization, or other human system describes the combination of traditionally administrative personnel functions with acquisition and application of skills, knowledge and experience, Employee Relations and resource planning at various levels. The field draws upon concepts developed in Industrial/Organizational Psychology and System Theory. _____ has at least two related interpretations depending on context. The original usage derives from political economy and economics, where it was traditionally called labor, one of four factors of production although this perspective is changing as a function of new and ongoing research into more strategic approaches at national levels. This first usage is used more in terms of '_____ development', and can go beyond just organizations to the level of nations. The more traditional usage within corporations and businesses refers to the individuals within a firm or agency, and to the portion of the organization that deals with hiring, firing, training, and other personnel issues, typically referred to as `_____ management'.

   a. Human resource management
   b. Human resources
   c. Progressive discipline
   d. Bradford Factor

14. _____ is a legally declared inability or impairment of ability of an individual or organization to pay its creditors. Creditors may file a _____ petition against a debtor ('involuntary _____') in an effort to recoup a portion of what they are owed or initiate a restructuring. In the majority of cases, however, _____ is initiated by the debtor (a 'voluntary _____' that is filed by the insolvent individual or organization.)

   a. 1990 Clean Air Act
   b. 28-hour day
   c. 33 Strategies of War
   d. Bankruptcy

15. The _____ of a company or public agency is the corporate officer primarily responsible for managing the financial risks of the business or agency. This officer is also responsible for financial planning and record-keeping, as well as financial reporting to higher management. (In recent years, however, the role has expanded to encompass communicating financial performance and forecasts to the analyst community.)

   a. 33 Strategies of War
   b. Chief financial officer
   c. 1990 Clean Air Act
   d. 28-hour day

16. The United Nations _____ is an United Nations initiative to encourage businesses worldwide to adopt sustainable and socially responsible policies, and to report on their implementation. The _____ is a principle based framework for businesses, stating ten principles in the areas of human rights, labour, the environment and anti-corruption. Under the _____, companies are brought together with UN agencies, labour groups and civil society.

a. Global Compact
b. 33 Strategies of War
c. 1990 Clean Air Act
d. 28-hour day

17. The _____ is a concept from business management that was first described and popularized by Michael Porter in his 1985 best-seller, Competitive Advantage: Creating and Sustaining Superior Performance.

A _____ is a chain of activities. Products pass through all activities of the chain in order and at each activity the product gains some value. The chain of activities gives the products more added value than the sum of added values of all activities. It is important not to mix the concept of the _____ with the costs occurring throughout the activities.

a. Market development
b. Mass marketing
c. Customer relationship management
d. Value chain

18. The general definition of an _____ is an evaluation of a person, organization, system, process, project or product. _____s are performed to ascertain the validity and reliability of information; also to provide an assessment of a system's internal control. The goal of an _____ is to express an opinion on the person / organization/system (etc) in question, under evaluation based on work done on a test basis.
a. Audit committee
b. Audit
c. A Stake in the Outcome
d. Internal control

19. A _____ or transnational corporation is a corporation or enterprise that manages production or delivers services in more than one country. It can also be referred to as an international corporation.

The first modern _____ is generally thought to be the Dutch East India Company, established in 1602.

a. Financial Accounting Standards Board
b. Small and medium enterprises
c. Command center
d. Multinational corporation

Chapter 7. Strategy Implementation

20. An _____ is a mostly hierarchical concept of subordination of entities that collaborate and contribute to serve one common aim.

Organizations are a variant of clustered entities. The structure of an organization is usually set up in many a styles, dependent on their objectives and ambience.

a. Organizational development
b. Open shop
c. Informal organization
d. Organizational structure

21. In economics, _____ describes the state of a market with respect to competition.

- Perfect competition, in which the market consists of a very large number of firms producing a homogeneous product.
- Monopolistic competition where there are a large number of independent firms which have a very small proportion of the market share.
- Oligopoly, in which a market is dominated by a small number of firms which own more than 40% of the market share.
- Oligopsony, a market dominated by many sellers and a few buyers.
- Monopoly, where there is only one provider of a product or service.
- Natural monopoly, a monopoly in which economies of scale cause efficiency to increase continuously with the size of the firm. A firm is a natural monopoly if it is able to serve the entire market demand at a lower cost than any combination of two or more smaller, more specialized firms.
- Monopsony, when there is only one buyer in a market.

The imperfectly competitive structure is quite identical to the realistic market conditions where some monopolistic competitors, monopolists, oligopolists, and duopolists exist and dominate the market conditions. The elements of _____ include the number and size distribution of firms, entry conditions, and the extent of differentiation.

These somewhat abstract concerns tend to determine some but not all details of a specific concrete market system where buyers and sellers actually meet and commit to trade.

a. Market structure
b. Leading indicator
c. Deflation
d. Productivity management

Chapter 7. Strategy Implementation

22. _____ refers to the movement of cash into or out of a business or financial product. It is usually measured during a specified, finite period of time. Measurement of _____ can be used

- to determine a project's rate of return or value. The time of _____s into and out of projects are used as inputs in financial models such as internal rate of return, and net present value.
- to determine problems with a business's liquidity. Being profitable does not necessarily mean being liquid. A company can fail because of a shortage of cash, even while profitable.
- as an alternate measure of a business's profits when it is believed that accrual accounting concepts do not represent economic realities. For example, a company may be notionally profitable but generating little operational cash (as may be the case for a company that barters its products rather than selling for cash.) In such a case, the company may be deriving additional operating cash by issuing shares evaluating default risk, re-investment requirements, etc.

_____ is a generic term used differently depending on the context. It may be defined by users for their own purposes.

a. Sweat equity
b. Cash flow
c. Gross profit
d. Gross profit margin

23. A _____ is a professional in the field of project management. _____s can have the responsibility of the planning, execution, and closing of any project, typically relating to construction industry, architecture, computer networking, telecommunications or software development.

Many other fields in the production, design and service industries also have _____s.

a. Project engineer
b. Project management
c. Work package
d. Project manager

24. _____ is understood as a business unit within the overall corporate identity which is distinguishable from other business because it serves a defined external market where management can conduct strategic planning in relation to products and markets. When companies become really large, they are best thought of as being composed of a number of businesses (or _____s.)

In the broader domain of strategic management, the phrase '_____' came into use in the 1960s, largely as a result of General Electric's many units.

a. Switching cost
b. Strategic group
c. Strategic drift
d. Strategic business unit

25. A _____ researches, selects, develops, and places a company's products.

A _____ considers numerous factors such as target demographic, the products offered by the competition, and how well the product fits in with the company's business model. Generally, a _____ manages one or more tangible products.

a. 1990 Clean Air Act
b. 28-hour day
c. 33 Strategies of War
d. Product manager

Chapter 8. Strategic Control and Restructuring

1. The _____ of 2002 (Pub.L. 107-204, 116 Stat. 745, enacted July 30, 2002), also known as the Public Company Accounting Reform and Investor Protection Act of 2002 and commonly called Sarbanes-Oxley, Sarbox or SOX, is a United States federal law enacted on July 30, 2002, as a reaction to a number of major corporate and accounting scandals including those affecting Enron, Tyco International, Adelphia, Peregrine Systems and WorldCom.

   a. Fair Labor Standards Act
   b. Sarbanes-Oxley Act of 2002
   c. Letter of credit
   d. Sarbanes-Oxley Act

2. The _____, also known as the Public Company Accounting Reform and Investor Protection Act of 2002 and commonly called Sarbanes-Oxley, Sarbox or SOX, is a United States federal law enacted on July 30, 2002, as a reaction to a number of major corporate and accounting scandals including those affecting Enron, Tyco International, Adelphia, Peregrine Systems and WorldCom.

   a. Letter of credit
   b. Munn v. Illinois
   c. MacPherson v. Buick Motor Co.
   d. Sarbanes-Oxley Act of 2002

3. _____ is one of the managerial functions like planning, organizing, staffing and directing. It is an important function because it helps to check the errors and to take the corrective action so that deviation from standards are minimized and stated goals of the organization are achieved in desired manner. According to modern concepts, _____ is a foreseeing action whereas earlier concept of _____ was used only when errors were detected. _____ in management means setting standards, measuring actual performance and taking corrective action.

   a. Decision tree pruning
   b. Turnover
   c. Schedule of reinforcement
   d. Control

4. The _____ is a chart that had been created by Bruce Henderson for the Boston Consulting Group in 1970 to help corporations with analyzing their business units or product lines. This helps the company allocate resources and is used as an analytical tool in brand marketing, product management, strategic management, and portfolio analysis. _____

   To use the chart, analysts plot a scatter graph to rank the business units (or products) on the basis of their relative market shares and growth rates.

   a. Marketing plan
   b. Marketing strategy
   c. Market segment
   d. BCG matrix

Chapter 8. Strategic Control and Restructuring

5. _____ , also referred to simply as a 'public offering' or 'flotation,' is when a company issues common stock or shares to the public for the first time. They are often issued by smaller, younger companies seeking capital to expand, but can also be done by large privately-owned companies looking to become publicly traded.

In an _____ the issuer may obtain the assistance of an underwriting firm, which helps it determine what type of security to issue (common or preferred), best offering price and time to bring it to market.

   a. Unemployment insurance
   b. Occupational Safety and Health Administration
   c. Outsourcing
   d. Initial public offering

6. The _____ of a company or public agency is the corporate officer primarily responsible for managing the financial risks of the business or agency. This officer is also responsible for financial planning and record-keeping, as well as financial reporting to higher management. (In recent years, however, the role has expanded to encompass communicating financial performance and forecasts to the analyst community.)
   a. 33 Strategies of War
   b. 28-hour day
   c. Chief financial officer
   d. 1990 Clean Air Act

7. _____ is a legally declared inability or impairment of ability of an individual or organization to pay its creditors. Creditors may file a _____ petition against a debtor ('involuntary _____') in an effort to recoup a portion of what they are owed or initiate a restructuring. In the majority of cases, however, _____ is initiated by the debtor (a 'voluntary _____' that is filed by the insolvent individual or organization.)
   a. Bankruptcy
   b. 28-hour day
   c. 33 Strategies of War
   d. 1990 Clean Air Act

8. _____ describes the situation when output from (or information about the result of) an event or phenomenon in the past will influence the same event/phenomenon in the present or future. When an event is part of a chain of cause-and-effect that forms a circuit or loop, then the event is said to 'feed back' into itself.

_____ is also a synonym for:

- _____ signal; the information about the initial event that is the basis for subsequent modification of the event.
- _____ loop; the causal path that leads from the initial generation of the _____ signal to the subsequent modification of the event.

_____ is a mechanism, process or signal that is looped back to control a system within itself. Such a loop is called a _____ loop.

a. Feedback
b. Feedback loop
c. 1990 Clean Air Act
d. Positive feedback

9. _____ is a concept in ethics with several meanings. It is often used synonymously with such concepts as responsibility, answerability, enforcement, blameworthiness, liability and other terms associated with the expectation of account-giving. As an aspect of governance, it has been central to discussions related to problems in both the public and private (corporation) worlds.
   a. Usury
   b. A Stake in the Outcome
   c. A4e
   d. Accountability

10. The United Nations _____ is an United Nations initiative to encourage businesses worldwide to adopt sustainable and socially responsible policies, and to report on their implementation. The _____ is a principle based framework for businesses, stating ten principles in the areas of human rights, labour, the environment and anti-corruption. Under the _____, companies are brought together with UN agencies, labour groups and civil society.
    a. 33 Strategies of War
    b. 28-hour day
    c. 1990 Clean Air Act
    d. Global Compact

11. The general definition of an _____ is an evaluation of a person, organization, system, process, project or product. _____s are performed to ascertain the validity and reliability of information; also to provide an assessment of a system's internal control. The goal of an _____ is to express an opinion on the person / organization/system (etc) in question, under evaluation based on work done on a test basis.

Chapter 8. Strategic Control and Restructuring

a. Audit committee
b. A Stake in the Outcome
c. Internal control
d. Audit

12. _____ generally refers to a list of all planned expenses and revenues. It is a plan for saving and spending. A _____ is an important concept in microeconomics, which uses a _____ line to illustrate the trade-offs between two or more goods.
    a. 1990 Clean Air Act
    b. 33 Strategies of War
    c. 28-hour day
    d. Budget

13. In finance, a _____ or accounting ratio is a ratio of two selected numerical values taken from an enterprise's financial statements. There are many standard ratios used to try to evaluate the overall financial condition of a corporation or other organization. _____s may be used by managers within a firm, by current and potential shareholders (owners) of a firm, and by a firm's creditors.
    a. Return on sales
    b. Return on equity
    c. Rate of return
    d. Financial ratio

14. _____ is, in very basic words, a position a firm occupies against its competitors.

According to Michael Porter, the three methods for creating a sustainable _____ are through:

1. Cost leadership

2. Differentiation

3. Focus (economics)

   a. 28-hour day
   b. Theory Z
   c. 1990 Clean Air Act
   d. Competitive Advantage

Chapter 8. Strategic Control and Restructuring

15. _____ is a term used to describe any moral, political that stresses human interdependence and the importance of a collective, rather than the importance of separate individuals. Collectivists focus on community and society, and seek to give priority to group goals over individual goals. The philosophical underpinnings of _____ are for some related to holism or organicism - the view that the whole is greater than the sum of its parts/pieces.
    a. Collectivism
    b. Collaborative methods
    c. 1990 Clean Air Act
    d. 28-hour day

16. _____ of the learning curve effect and the closely related experience curve effect express the relationship between equations for experience and efficiency or between efficiency gains and investment in the effort. The experience of 'learning curves' was first observed by the 19th Century German psychologist Hermann Ebbinghaus according to the difficulty of memorizing varying numbers of verbal stimuli, and subsequent learning about the complex processes of learning are discussed in the

The rule used for representing the learning curve effect states that the more times a task has been performed, the less time will be required on each subsequent iteration.

    a. Spatial Decision Support Systems
    b. Distribution
    c. Point biserial correlation coefficient
    d. Models

17. _____ is the corporate management term for the act of reorganizing the legal, ownership, operational, or other structures of a company for the purpose of making it more profitable, or better organized for its present needs. Alternate reasons for _____ include a change of ownership or ownership structure, demerger repositioning debt _____ and financial _____.
    a. Market value added
    b. Restructuring
    c. Net worth
    d. Market value

18. In business and accounting, _____s are everything of value that is owned by a person or company. Any property or object of value that one possesses, usually considered as applicable to the payment of one's debts is considered an _____. Simplistically stated, _____s are things of value that can be readily converted into cash.

a. A4e
b. Asset
c. A Stake in the Outcome
d. AAAI

19. _____ is the use of control systems (such as numerical control, programmable logic control, and other industrial control systems), in concert with other applications of information technology (such as computer-aided technologies [CAD, CAM, CAx]), to control industrial machinery and processes, reducing the need for human intervention. In the scope of industrialization, _____ is a step beyond mechanization. Whereas mechanization provided human operators with machinery to assist them with the physical requirements of work, _____ greatly reduces the need for human sensory and mental requirements as well.
   a. A4e
   b. Automation
   c. AAAI
   d. A Stake in the Outcome

20. _____ is the temporary suspension or permanent termination of employment of an employee or (more commonly) a group of employees for business reasons, such as the decision that certain positions are no longer necessary or a business slow-down or interruption in work. Originally the term '_____' referred exclusively to a temporary interruption in work, as when factory work cyclically falls off. However, in recent times the term can also refer to the permanent elimination of a position.
   a. Layoff
   b. Retirement
   c. Termination of employment
   d. Wrongful dismissal

21. A _____ is a new organization or entity formed by a split from a larger one, such as a television series based on a pre-existing one, or a new company formed from a university research group or business incubator. In literature, especially in milieu-based popular fictional book series like mysteries, westerns, fantasy or science fiction, the term sub-series is generally used instead of _____, but with essentially the same meaning.

_____s as a descriptive term can also include a dissenting faction of a membership organization, a sect of a cult, or a denomination of a church.

   a. 28-hour day
   b. 33 Strategies of War
   c. 1990 Clean Air Act
   d. Spin-off

Chapter 8. Strategic Control and Restructuring

22. The _____ is the labour pool in employment. It is generally used to describe those working for a single company or industry, but can also apply to a geographic region like a city, country, state, etc. The term generally excludes the employers or management, and implies those involved in manual labour.
    a. Pink-collar worker
    b. Workforce
    c. Division of labour
    d. Work-life balance

23. In general, a _____ is an arrangement to provide people with an income when they are no longer earning a regular income from employment.

The terms retirement plan or superannuation refer to a _____ granted upon retirement . Retirement plans may be set up by employers, insurance companies, the government or other institutions such as employer associations or trade unions.

   a. Pension insurance contract
   b. Pension
   c. State Compensation Insurance Fund
   d. Wage

24. A _____ is an investment transaction by which an entire company or a controlling part of the stock of a company is sold. A firm 'buys out' a company to take control of it. A _____ can take the form of a leveraged _____, a venture capital _____ or a management _____.
   a. Shareholder value
   b. Sweat equity
   c. Buyout
   d. Gross profit

25. A _____ occurs when a financial sponsor acquires a controlling interest in a company's equity and where a significant percentage of the purchase price is financed through leverage (borrowing.) The assets of the acquired company are used as collateral for the borrowed capital, sometimes with assets of the acquiring company. The bonds or other paper issued for _____s are commonly considered not to be investment grade because of the significant risks involved.
   a. Limited partners
   b. Venture capital
   c. Growth capital
   d. Leveraged buyout

26. _____ is the process of estimation in unknown situations. Prediction is a similar, but more general term. Both can refer to estimation of time series, cross-sectional or longitudinal data.
   a. Forecasting
   b. 33 Strategies of War
   c. 1990 Clean Air Act
   d. 28-hour day

27. _____ is a form of corporate self-regulation integrated into a business model. Ideally, _____ policy would function as a built-in, self-regulating mechanism whereby business would monitor and ensure their adherence to law, ethical standards, and international norms. Business would embrace responsibility for the impact of their activities on the environment, consumers, employees, communities, stakeholders and all other members of the public sphere.
   a. 1990 Clean Air Act
   b. 28-hour day
   c. 33 Strategies of War
   d. Corporate social responsibility

28. The term '_____' refers to the concept of collecting information and attempting to spot a pattern in the information. In some fields of study, the term '_____' has more formally-defined meanings.

In project management _____ is a mathematical technique that uses historical results to predict future outcome.

   a. Stepwise regression
   b. Least squares
   c. Regression analysis
   d. Trend analysis

29. _____ is one of the most general and applicable methods of analytical thinking, depending only on the division of a problem, decision or situation into a sufficient number of separate cases. Analysing each such case individually may be enough to resolve the initial question. The principle of _____ is invoked in the celebrated remark of Sherlock Holmes, to the effect that when one has eliminated the impossible, what remains must be true, however unlikely that seems.
   a. Validity
   b. Case analysis
   c. Simplification
   d. 1990 Clean Air Act

30. In economics, business, retail, and accounting, a _____ is the value of money that has been used up to produce something, and hence is not available for use anymore. In economics, a _____ is an alternative that is given up as a result of a decision. In business, the _____ may be one of acquisition, in which case the amount of money expended to acquire it is counted as _____.
   a. Cost overrun
   b. Fixed costs
   c. Cost allocation
   d. Cost

31. _____ Management is the succession of strategies used by management as a product goes through its _____. The conditions in which a product is sold changes over time and must be managed as it moves through its succession of stages.

The _____ goes through many phases, involves many professional disciplines, and requires many skills, tools and processes.

   a. Golden handshake
   b. Job hunting
   c. Product life cycle
   d. Strategic Alliance

32. _____ is an organization's process of defining its strategy and making decisions on allocating its resources to pursue this strategy, including its capital and people. Various business analysis techniques can be used in _____, including SWOT analysis (Strengths, Weaknesses, Opportunities, and Threats) and PEST analysis (Political, Economic, Social, and Technological analysis) or STEER analysis involving Socio-cultural, Technological, Economic, Ecological, and Regulatory factors and EPISTEL (Environment, Political, Informatic, Social, Technological, Economic and Legal)

_____ is the formal consideration of an organization's future course. All _____ deals with at least one of three key questions:

   1. 'What do we do?'
   2. 'For whom do we do it?'
   3. 'How do we excel?'

In business _____, the third question is better phrased 'How can we beat or avoid competition?'. (Bradford and Duncan, page 1.)

a. 33 Strategies of War
b. 28-hour day
c. 1990 Clean Air Act
d. Strategic planning

ANSWER KEY

Chapter 1
1. d 2. c 3. b 4. c 5. b 6. c 7. a 8. a 9. c 10. d
11. c 12. d 13. b 14. d 15. d 16. c 17. a 18. d

Chapter 2
1. b 2. d 3. b 4. a 5. d 6. a 7. d 8. c 9. b 10. d
11. a 12. d 13. a 14. a 15. b 16. d 17. d 18. c 19. d 20. a
21. c 22. d 23. b 24. c 25. a 26. a

Chapter 3
1. c 2. a 3. d 4. b 5. d 6. b 7. b 8. c 9. d 10. a
11. d 12. a 13. c 14. d 15. d 16. a 17. c 18. d 19. a 20. c
21. d 22. d 23. d 24. d 25. a 26. d 27. d 28. d 29. c 30. a
31. d 32. a 33. d 34. c 35. c 36. d 37. d 38. a 39. a 40. a
41. c 42. d 43. d

Chapter 4
1. d 2. d 3. d 4. b 5. d 6. d 7. c 8. a 9. d 10. b

Chapter 5
1. b 2. c 3. a 4. d 5. a 6. c 7. d 8. d 9. a 10. b
11. a 12. d 13. d 14. b 15. d 16. d 17. d 18. d 19. d 20. d
21. d 22. d 23. a 24. d 25. d 26. d 27. d 28. c

Chapter 6
1. a 2. b 3. b 4. a 5. c 6. c 7. b 8. d 9. c 10. d
11. a 12. c 13. d 14. a 15. d 16. d 17. d

Chapter 7
1. c 2. d 3. b 4. d 5. b 6. d 7. d 8. d 9. b 10. c
11. d 12. d 13. b 14. d 15. b 16. a 17. d 18. b 19. d 20. d
21. a 22. b 23. d 24. d 25. d

Chapter 8
1. d 2. d 3. d 4. d 5. d 6. c 7. a 8. a 9. d 10. d
11. d 12. d 13. d 14. d 15. a 16. d 17. b 18. b 19. b 20. a
21. d 22. b 23. b 24. c 25. d 26. a 27. d 28. d 29. b 30. d
31. c 32. d

www.ingramcontent.com/pod-product-compliance
Lightning Source LLC
Chambersburg PA
CBHW080743250426
43671CB00038B/2845